HARRIET TUBMAN

Troll Associates

HARRIET TUBMAN

by Francene Sabin

Illustrated by Hal Frenck

Troll Associates

Library of Congress Cataloging in Publication Data

Sabin, Francene.
    Harriet Tubman.

    Summary: A biography of the black woman who escaped
from slavery and became a well-known figure in the
underground railroad as she led scores of slaves north
to freedom.
        1. Tubman, Harriet, 1815?-1913—Juvenile literature.
2. Slaves—United States—Biography—Juvenile literature.
3. Afro-Americans—Biography—Juvenile literature.
4. Underground railroad—Juvenile literature.
[1. Tubman, Harriet, 1815?-1913.   2. Slaves.   3. Afro-
Americans—Biography]   I. Frenck, Hal, ill.   II. Title.
E44.T82S23   1984   973'.0496024 [B] [92]   84-2667
ISBN 0-8167-0158-X (lib. bdg.)
ISBN 0-8167-0159-8 (pbk.)

Harriet Tubman, born a slave, was a woman of extraordinary courage and faith. She was known to nineteenth-century slaves as "Moses," and like the biblical Moses, she helped to lead her people to freedom. And when slavery was at last abolished, she fought on to bring justice and equality to all people.

Harriet Tubman, the sixth of eleven children, was born around 1820. Her parents, Ben Ross and Harriet Green, were slaves on the plantation of Edward Brodas, in Dorchester County, Maryland. The exact date of her birth is not known because no records were kept of the birth of slaves.

Slaves were chattel, which means they were considered to be property, like a bale of cotton or a farm animal. Slaves were not allowed to be legally married, go to church, or have any kind of education. Slaves could be bought and sold and treated cruelly by their masters. This was the kind of world into which Harriet was born.

The little girl's home was a one-room shack with no furniture. The family slept on rags laid on the floor. Their food was mostly corn mush, eaten right from the pot in which it was cooked. They had no dishes, but scooped out their food with pieces of stone or oyster shells. Their workday started before dawn and lasted until dark. The only day they didn't work was Sunday.

Like most slave children, Harriet began to earn her keep when she was just three years old. It was then that she was put to work, running errands for the Brodas family. Sometimes she had to carry messages as far as ten miles away. And she was punished if she took too long getting back.

Then, at the age of six, she was hired out by her master to a neighboring family. Though Harriet was sick with measles, they sent her into an ice-cold river to check animal traps. She became very ill and had to be sent home.

Harriet survived, through her mother's devotion and care, only to be sent to work for a family that treated her even more cruelly. These people made her work all day and night. Again, Harriet fell ill. And again, her mother had to nurse the sickly girl back to health.

At the age of nine, Harriet was put to work as a field hand, planting, weeding, hoeing, and harvesting the crops. Harriet also split logs with an axe, hauled wood, and did other backbreaking jobs.

The young slave girl labored as hard as she could. She was constantly afraid of being sold by the master and sent far away from her family.

Harriet never forgot how two of her older sisters had been sold to slave owners farther south. Being "sold South" was the most terrifying threat to the slaves in Virginia and Maryland. When it did happen, families were torn apart, never to be reunited. And the cotton and rice plantations in the deep South were many times worse than the Virginia and Maryland plantations.

While Harriet's body grew strong from her daily labor in the fields, her mind was busy with the important things she was learning from the older slaves. Harriet learned Bible stories and prayers, and she felt strengthened by them. The story of Moses, leading the Israelites from slavery, was a particularly important one. The slaves in the American South prayed for a Moses to lead them to freedom.

Harriet believed deeply in the message of the Bible—that all people were equal in the eyes of God. And she believed that God would ease the burden on her people.

Harriet also learned the stories of the brave American slaves who fought for freedom. She heard of Nat Turner, who led a revolt of slaves. And she learned of Tice Davids, who ran away from his plantation and seemed to have magically escaped to the North. The runaway, it was said, must have traveled along an underground railroad to escape his pursuers. Again and again, Harriet heard about the marvelous "underground railroad" that made it possible for slaves to escape.

Of course, there was really no train that ran underground. As Harriet quickly found out, the underground railroad was actually a group of people who opposed slavery. Some of these people hid runaway slaves on their property, gave them food, and directed them to the next safe hiding place. These people were called stationmasters. The hiding places were called stations, or depots.

Those people who led the runaways from one depot to another were called conductors. The runaways, themselves, were known as passengers, or parcels. As young Harriet listened to these stories, she vowed that one day she, too, would take the ride to freedom.

When Harriet was fifteen, she suffered a terrible injury. One evening she was in a local store when the slave of a nearby farmer came in. Soon after, the farmer entered the store and ordered the slave back to the fields.

The slave didn't move, and the farmer threatened to whip him. Suddenly, the slave ran to the door. The farmer picked up a heavy lead weight and threw it. The piece of metal missed the slave but struck Harriet in the head. She dropped to the floor, unconscious.

For months, the girl lay near death. Then, slowly, she recovered. But the effects of the injury stayed with Harriet all her life. She always had a deep scar in her forehead. And every now and then she would fall into a deep sleep that lasted about fifteen minutes.

After the accident, Mr. Brodas tried to sell Harriet. But she didn't want to be separated from her family. So each time a buyer was brought to see her, Harriet pretended to have one of her sleeping spells or acted very stupid. Her act always succeeded.

Harriet returned to work in the fields as soon as she was able. But she was more determined than ever to be free. She even hoped to buy her freedom someday.

In 1844, Harriet married a free black man named John Tubman. She was allowed to marry him because he was free. Harriet hoped he would help her get away to the North. But the marriage did not work out.

In 1849, Mr. Brodas died, and the slaves heard they were going to be sold. Harriet knew she must now escape. She sneaked off to the home of a white woman who had offered to help her. The woman gave her a note and directions to a house miles away. When Harriet got there, she handed the note to the woman of the house.

The woman read the note, then gave Harriet a broom and told her to sweep the yard. Suddenly, Harriet understood— nobody would suspect that a black woman working openly was a runaway slave.

That night Harriet was hidden in a wagon of hay and taken to another town. She was passed this way from station to station of the underground railroad, until she crossed into Pennsylvania and was free.

But Harriet's fight for freedom had just begun. Now she wanted others to taste the freedom she found so sweet. In the next few years she succeeded in bringing her elderly parents, her sister, brothers, nieces, and nephews to freedom.

She also led more than three hundred other slaves to freedom. In doing so, Harriet Tubman became the most famous and successful conductor on the underground railroad. For this, she earned the title of Moses.

Harriet's success was due to her patience, her cleverness, and her boundless energy. Although there was a forty-thousand dollar reward for her capture, she was never caught.

She didn't stop leading slaves to freedom until the Civil War started in 1861. And then, Harriet turned her energies to work as a scout and spy for the Union Army. She also served as a nurse, tending the sick and wounded of both the Union and the Confederacy.

After the Civil War, Harriet Tubman settled near the home she had bought for her parents in Auburn, New York. She married a man named Nelson Davis and began to enjoy her first days of peace and untroubled family life.

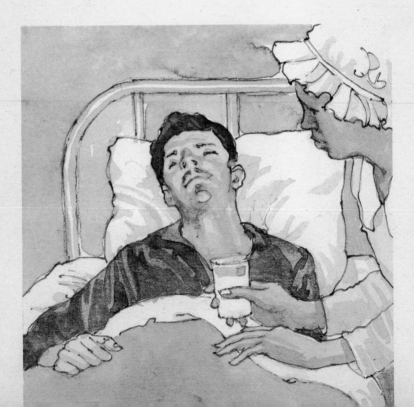

But the woman called Moses could not rest for long. Wherever she found injustice, she tried to make it right. She became a spokesperson for women's rights, traveling from place to place, making speeches for the cause.

At the same time, Harriet continued her fight against racial injustice. The Civil War had put an official end to slavery, but it had not made life much better for most black Americans. They were still the victims of many forms of discrimination.

Harriet was especially concerned about elderly former slaves. When slavery ended, they were thrown off the land where they had worked. They had nowhere to go and no way to make a living. For these people, Harriet worked to establish a home in Auburn, New York.

Another of Harriet Tubman's great concerns was for the education of black children. Only through education would they be able to achieve a better life. So she began a crusade to raise funds to build and staff schools. She kept at this and her other causes for the rest of her life.

The flame that burned in Harriet Tubman never grew weak. Until her death, on March 10, 1913, at the age of ninety-three, she continued to fight for freedom and equality. And when she died, Harriet Tubman was honored with a military funeral. No one deserved it more than the woman called Moses.